Basic
LEARNI

HOW TO GIVE

A Classroom Talk

TRILOBYTE PRESS

Basic Concepts
LEARNING GUIDES©

How to Give a Classroom Talk

First published in 1993 by
TRILOBYTE PRESS
1486 Willowdown Road
Oakville, ON
Canada, L6L 1X3

Printed by Pocket Press

Canadian Cataloguing in Publication Data

Main entry under title:

How to give a classroom talk

(Basic concepts learning guides)

Based on How to succeed at college by Danton H. O'Day.

ISBN 1-895482-16-X

1. Public Speaking. I. Series.

PN4121.H68 1993 808.5'1 C93-094674-X

Basic Concepts
LEARNING GUIDES©

HOW TO GIVE A CLASSROOM TALK

TABLE OF CONTENTS

Chapter One. INTRODUCTION...1

Giving a classroom talk...1

One talk leads to another...2

Understand what is expected...3

Chapter Two. ORGANIZATION IS THE KEY...5

How to organize a talk...5

The introduction sets the stage...6

Audio-visual aids help...7

Set the limits of your talk...12

The discussion...13

Concluding your talk...13

Chapter Three. MAKING OVERHEADS: QUICK & EASY...15

Audio-visual aids will improve your talk...15

Start simply...17

Making professional overheads...18
What about graphs and figures?...20

Chapter Four. READING OR ROTE?...27
How do I present my talk...27
Use cue cards to remember...28
Don't panic if you forget something...29
Write down your introductory statements...30
Write down important points...30
Make photocopies of your overheads...31

Chapter Five. IMPROVING YOUR TALK...33
Make it interesting...33
Using humor...34
Humor is not just telling jokes...35
Using audiovisual aids effectively...37
Using overheads effectively...38
More helpful hints for using overheads...40

Chapter Five. A SHORT REVIEW...41
Presenting a talk: summary...41

Chapter One

INTRODUCTION

GIVING A CLASSROOM TALK

The first time you are asked to give an oral presentation you will probably experience some fear. Standing up in front of a group of your peers and your instructor to give an oral presentation can be scary. You may worry that you won't be able to remember what you are supposed to say, that you will panic or that your classmates will act like the proverbial lions and tear you to shreds.

During your school years you will occasionally have to speak in front of an audience. Simply speaking up during class to ask you instructor a question is going to take some nerve. But at some point in most student's careers, it will be necessary to present a prepared talk. These oral presentations may be short summaries on a subject to get a discussion going in a group or tutorial. Or, they may be full-fledged seminars lasting up to half an hour or so.

The bottom line is, most students are afraid of talking in front of their class. So, welcome to the club.

In this booklet, we will take a step-by-step approach to presenting a class talk. In addition to discussing the mechanics of giving oral presentations, we will deal with specific problems that students face in making them. Ways to improve upon your oral presentations will be given and techniques to liven up your talk will be discussed.

ONE TALK LEADS TO ANOTHER

It's important to realize that during your lifetime you likely will be called upon many times to give a talk. If you join a club and become a member of the club's executive, you will have to speak to the other members about proposed plans, the budget or any number of other topics. Depending on your job after you graduate, you may be required to make reports on your progress from time to time. If you go to college or university, you will face the prospect of presenting numerous talks to your professors and fellow students. The skills you learn here will be transferable to any of these other situations. So public speaking is a skill many would like to have. If you learn the basis of giving a good classroom talk, it's only a short jump to becoming a top-notch public speaker.

UNDERSTAND WHAT IS EXPECTED

Just like any of your responsibilities as a student, you must understand what is required of you when an oral presentation is to be given. At the very least, this means you must know the following things:

- how long you are supposed to talk,
- the format of your talk, and,
- the subject of the talk.

Like a written report, an oral presentation must be organized. It must be a logical progression of ideas with an Introduction, Discussion and Conclusions. Often, in fact, the oral report will be coupled with the submission of a written report. In such cases, the oral part will simply be a short distillation of the paper. Let's look at the basic organization of a classroom talk or seminar and then discuss how modifications can be made to this format as required.

NOTES

Chapter Two

ORGANIZATION IS THE KEY

HOW TO ORGANIZE A TALK

In its most basic form, a seminar is put together in the same way as you would put together a written report. Just as book reports, lab reports and essays are examples of the diverse types of written reports that you will produce in your school years, so the structure of a class talk or other oral presentation can vary based on the type of information you are trying to communicate or the group of people that you are speaking to.

In general, a classroom talk will consist of:

- an *Introduction* to the subject,
- a *Discussion* of the relevant material, and,
- some *Conclusions.*

Often you will have to field questions from the audience about your talk. Such questions commonly come at the end but they may also be permitted, and are sometimes necessary, during the talk. If you don't want to be interrupted during your presentation, you can request that the audience wait until you are finished before they ask questions.

THE INTRODUCTION SETS THE STAGE

Of course you have to begin at the beginning. In the Introduction you will set the stage for your talk. First, give the title of your seminar. For example, you might begin by saying, "The topic of today's talk is, The Role of Television in a Student's Life." Then you would take time to explain why this topic is important and what the purpose of your talk is. Give any relevant background information to let the audience know why the subject is important.

In providing background information, it is not essential to review in detail what your audience should already know. It is expected that all of the students will have such information at their fingertips. Your aim is to remind your audience about such information, then focus upon any specific details of which they may not be aware. For example, if you were going to introduce the literature of Margaret Atwood and her work had been covered earlier in your course, you would not use your old course notes as an Introduction. You would mention the major points covered previously in the course. Then impress upon your audience any new background information they may not be aware of and how your material will extend their knowledge.

It is important for you to clearly set the stage for your talk. To tell your audience exactly what you intend to do and why. Be affirmative! If you lose them in the Introduction, you've probably lost them for the duration of your talk.

AUDIO-VISUAL AIDS HELP

If you are using audio-visual aids, you should have an outline of your talk available to present to your audience. This can be written on part of the blackboard. If possible, it will look more professional if it is presented as an overhead or slide. Later in this booklet, we'll discuss making simple but professional looking overheads and slides. Suffice to say, it is simple to make great audio-visual aids with little effort at all. On the following pages are examples of good and bad outlines that could be presented to your audience.

Later we'll discuss how to prepare effective audio-visual and other aids. First, let's first look at an example of a bad overhead.

Example of an outline that is too detailed

GROWTH OF THE HUMAN BODY

I. INTRODUCTION

- **A. What is growth?**
  1. **Growth in size and number**
  2. **Growth in volume**
  3. **Increase in cell numbers**
- **B. When does it start?**
  1. **Embryonic growth**
  2. **Growth and infancy**
  3. **Growth and pubescence**
  4. **Growth and aging**
- **C. When does it end?**
  1. **Is there growth after adulthood?**
  2. **Can we measure when growth stops?**
- **D. Growth and Aging**
  1. **Do old people grow?**
  2. **Should we measure growth the same?**

II. DISCUSSION

- **A. Ways to measure growth.**
  1. **The Slim-fast versus Non-diet assay.**
  2. **Is weight gain equal to growth?**
  3. **Cells or tissues?**

GROWTH OF THE HUMAN BODY
Continued

B. Errors in growth measurement
  1. How much is too much?
  2. Inborn errors
  3. Unknown errors

C. Is Growth the same as development?
  1. When are they the same?
  2. When are they different?

D. Models of growth
  1. The two classic models
  2. A new model

III. CONCLUSIONS

A. Understanding growth and its implications
  1. A call for new standards
  2. More precise tools needed

B. Models for the future
  1. The holistic growth model
  2. Implications for the future

What thoughts ran through your mind as you examined the overheads presented on the previous two pages? What did you learn by looking at this approach to presenting an outline during the introduction to the talk on *The Growth of the Human Body?* It's safe to say, if you were in the audience of a talk that started with this outline, you probably would think about some or most of the following:

- Too much detail is provided
- The details confuse the overall plan
- The details suggest there will be repetition
- There's too much to read
- There's too much for a single overhead
- The speaker will likely try to cover too much
- The talk will be too complex
- The talk will be too long
- Get me outta here!

The last sentence says it all. A poorly conceived overhead or other audio-visual aid can quickly turn your audience off. But this doesn't have to happen.

The rule of thumb for all presentations and parts thereof is KISS: Keep It Simple, Stupid. So a simple approach that would orient your audience sufficiently is shown in the overhead outline presented on the next page.

An example of an overhead for a basic talk outline

GROWTH OF THE HUMAN BODY

I. INTRODUCTION

A. What is growth?
B. When does it start and end?
C. Growth and Aging

II. DISCUSSION

A. Measuring growth.
B. Errors in measurement
C. Is it the same as development?
D. Some Examples

III. CONCLUSIONS

A. Understanding growth
B. Models for the future

There are some important points to make about this introductory overhead:

- It is complete, but not too detailed
- It tells your audience what you will cover
- It fits on a single overhead easily
- It is well laid out
- It is quick and easy to read

SET THE LIMITS OF YOUR TALK

In your introduction, in addition to telling your audience the subject and approach you will take, you should also set the limits of your talk. You'll never have time to talk about everything on the subject you have chosen. More importantly, even if you did, few would be interested in hearing it all. People have a limited attention span. A talk that is too long is usually a bad talk.

Tell your audience what you will focus upon and, if necessary, what you will be leaving out. List the points that you will be discussing. If this is only a short talk, you may not be employing audio-visual aids. If such aids are required, then you should use them effectively to make your points as outlined above.

THE DISCUSSION

In the Discussion you will give the arguments and evidence that will support your final Conclusions. This information must be presented in a logical sequence and it must deal with the goals you set in your Introduction. You must have information to back up your arguments (e.g., in our example, you might make specific quotations from Ms. Atwood's books). Make sure that any points you raised in the Introduction are covered in the Discussion.

When you raise a point that is especially controversial, you should make sure that you have supporting arguments against the currently held views. If necessary, you should also be ready to defend those views in the questions that follow your concluding remarks.

CONCLUDING YOUR TALK

In the Conclusion, you will summarize what you have discussed. You will also reaffirm any strong convictions, if any, that have arisen. Your Conclusions must flow from your previous Discussion. It should answer any questions that you proposed in the Introduction. Sometimes you may use the Conclusions to propose some new ideas or thoughts for the future but they must be coherent and valid extensions of your earlier comments and ideas.

NOTES

Chapter Three

MAKING OVERHEADS: QUICK & EASY

AUDIO-VISUAL AIDS WILL IMPROVE YOUR TALK

Today, it's simple to pump up your classroom talk by using overheads. Those with photographic abilities may also consider making slides. Here we'll discuss the subject of audio-visual aids with the idea that you will use overheads. The techniques that are discussed can also be used in making slides. Overheads are generally more useful because they can be used in well-lit rooms. On the other hand, slides usually can only be shown in darkened rooms.

With the increasing availability of color photocopiers, it is no longer necessary to only use black and white overheads. However, we'll only discuss using overheads of one, or at most a few colors. It must be remembered that great audio-visual aids can enhance a good talk, but they can't save a poor one.

Some Uses of Audio-Visual Aids

- **They can illustrate difficult concepts**
- **They can orient your audience**
- **They help to keep you on track**
- **They add depth to your presentation**

START SIMPLY

In the simplest situation, it is possible to make overheads simply by writing on acetate or other plastic overhead sheets. If you print neatly, these will be more professional than writing the information on the blackboard. More importantly, it's usually easier to see overheads from the back.

If you print neatly and use a couple of different colored markers to emphasize or highlight specific details, your overheads will be more useful. Don't use too many colors or your overhead will look amateurish. Too much is as bad as too little.

As your teacher has probably done, you shouldn't uncover the complete overhead as soon as you present it. Otherwise, your audience will read on ahead and focus on issues you haven't covered yet. It can severely undermine your talk causing you to lose the attention of your audience. This is especially important for detailed lists of items or a series of steps in an argument or process. Instead, use a piece of opaque paper to reveal your overhead in stages as you talk about it. This forces your audience to stay with you.

Earlier we saw examples of a good and bad overhead. We discussed what was wrong with the bad one. We also reflected on the merits of the good one. But, we didn't discuss how to actually make a good overhead. Let's do that now.

HOW TO MAKE A GOOD OVERHEAD

1. Keep the information simple (KISS) by:

- using short phrases in point form, not sentences
- checking that your points are clearly stated
- not including every subtopic, just the major points.

2. Make it easy to read by:

- using large print
- leaving wide spaces between lines
- highlighting important names or items.

3. Make sure you don't stray into the margins. Otherwise you will continually have to shift the overhead around on the projection surface.

4. Try your overheads out beforehand to see how they look when projected.

MAKING PROFESSIONAL OVERHEADS

It's only a short step from writing out or drawing freehand on overhead sheets to making professional looking aids. What's even better: you don't have to be a genius to make great looking overheads. The photocopier can do all the work for you. If you have a computer, especially an IBM with Windows or an alternative word processing system or a Mac, you can make truly professional overheads.

If you don't use a computer for preparing reports or anything else except games, then you might not understand some of the terms that will be covered. At this stage of your life, you should be thinking seriously about employing computers in some aspects of your education. They aren't going to go away. What's more, many employers expect their employees to be able to use one.

Using your computer writing program, you simply type in the important material in the sequence you want. You can always re-arrange it later if you aren't pleased with the end result. If you use the Window's Write program for example, format this type using one of the easy to read fonts that come with the package such as Arena Condensed. Use the example of a good overhead in Chapter Two as a guide to arranging your information. Change the size of the fonts so that the image will be easy to read when projected.

Print out a copy and see if it meets your needs. If it does you now are ready to make an overhead. If you have a laser printer hooked up to computer, you can make the overhead by putting a piece of laser or photocopier overhead acetate material in the paper tray. The printer will print on the sheet as if it were paper. Use only proper overhead sheets designed for use in laser printers or photocopiers. Don't just stick any plastic overhead sheet into your laser printer or you could be in for trouble when it melts!

Most students won't have access to a laser printer. A dot matrix print on paper will serve as the basis of the overhead. In this case, the printed page will be transferred to an overhead sheet using a photocopier. Put the page to be photocopied on the copier and put the overhead sheet in the paper tray and make a copy. Use only proper copier overhead sheets, as indicated in the previous paragraph, for laser printing.

WHAT ABOUT GRAPHS AND FIGURES?

Printed lists are one thing, but what about graphs, tables, figures and complex drawings? Preparing these is also easy. With a few helpful hints you can also prepare them so they look fantastic rather than simply a copy of a page from your textbook.

Again, we begin with a word to the wise. Don't try to communicate too much information. Take some time and select a few images that you want to show. Also, if you limit the number, you will be able to spend more time on each one. This will ensure they look good.

We'll take an example of a graph and a more complex drawing to illustrate our points. On the next few pages, we will see a figure of the structure of the human ear that has been taken from a theoretical textbook. As you know, figures in textbooks are not designed for simple photocopying. In addition to the picture, there is surrounding text. The key to good overheads is to isolate the graphic.

MAKING AN OVERHEAD FROM A TEXTBOOK
A Step by Step Approach

1. Make a clear photocopy of the material.

Make photocopies of any figures that you want to work with (e.g., the human ear). If the photocopier has enlarge and reduce abilities, then you might want to increase or decrease the size of the figure.

2. Carefully cut-out the image you want.

Take those copied figures to an area where you can work on it. Carefully cut out the photocopied images.

3. Glue the image on a fresh piece of paper.

Center and glue the copied image on a clean piece of paper so that the background will appear white when you re-photocopy it.

4. Copy the image onto an overhead sheet.

You might want to make a regular copy as a test to make sure your image will come out properly. This can also be used for making notes for use in your talk as discussed later in this booklet.

This approach was used to generate our first example of the human ear. The image of the ear was trimmed of all surrounding text so only the drawing with its labels was left. It was centered and pasted on a clean piece of paper then rephotocopied. An overhead can now be made from it as detailed above. Let's see how it appears.

Example of a Cleaned Up Textbook Figure For Use as an Overhead

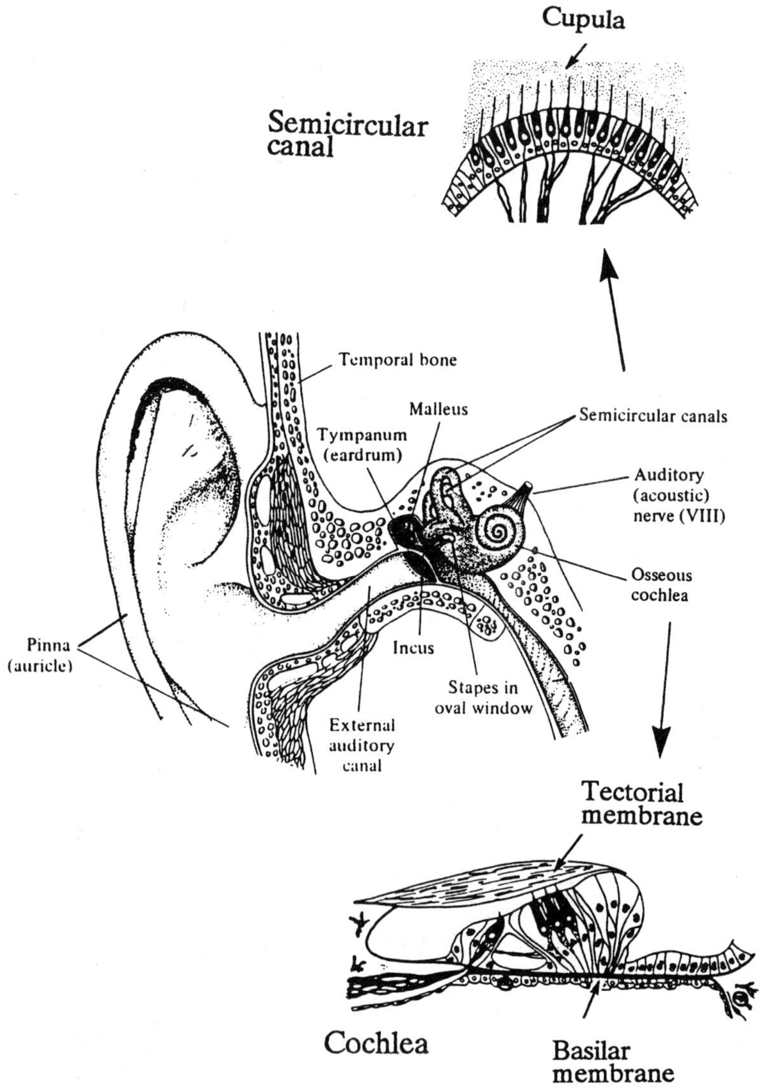

The previous overhead looks good and is more than acceptable for most presentations. In fact, most students don't even go this far. Most simply photocopy a full textbook page that contains their figure and use it. First of all the image is usually too small. In addition, it is surrounded by text. It looks sloppy and the text is distracting. On the other hand, if the picture is clear and large enough, such images can still be used to communicate useful information.

The point is anyone can simply copy a picture from a book and show it. We're trying to go a step further towards producing overheads that look good and that will be even better each time out.

So what is wrong with the picture on the previous page? For many, it contains too much information. If your class has already discussed the structure and function of the ear, then it may be good enough. If not, you need to orient your audience. In this case, you might just show part of the figure first, like this:

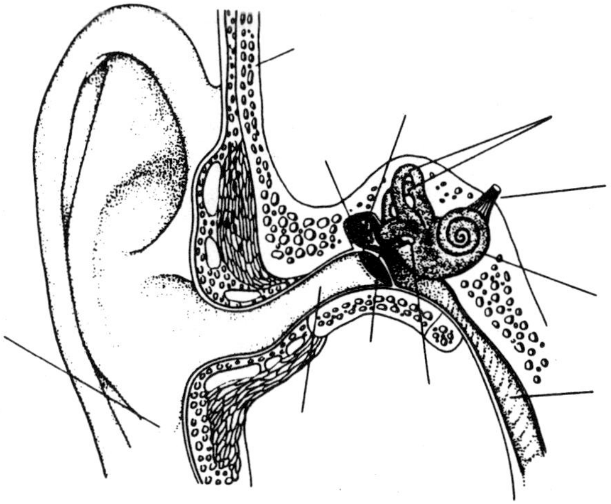

With the projected image on the screen, you could tell your audience about it by indicating the structures. Note that the names of the ear parts (e.g., Pinna, Incus, etc.) have been removed from the drawing. This was done by simply cutting up a photocopy and re-copying it minus the names. You can also use a white out product to eradicate names or structures and simplify your overhead.

As you talk, indicate the structures. You can also fill in the names of the structures as you point to them. If you are going to discuss one of the specific components in more detail, you could highlight it. For example, if you were going to talk about the role of the cochlea, you could color it in with an overhead marker. Do this beforehand and your overhead will look more interesting. If you have access to an enlarging photocopier, you could copy the cochlea from the original figure as a separate overhead. Again, just cut and paste and re-photocopy. Photocopy centers can do this for you if you take in the cleaned up image.

Here's how our cochlea would look:

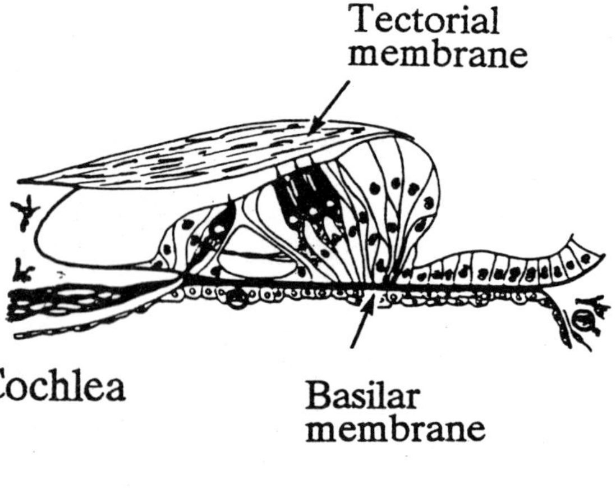

Cochlea

In summary, a little cutting and pasting can go a long way to improving your overheads. It only takes a few minutes more and it gives the image of professionalism. If time is short, then by all means just project a copy from a book or other source. After all you are trying to communicate information, it doesn't have to be beautiful. On the other hand, if you have the time, the few extra minutes spent on improving that communication of data can be very valuable.

Although we have only shown the process for a drawing, the ideas used above can also be employed for presenting graphs and tables from different publications. With graphs that are complex you can highlight the important line in a different color from the others (e.g., use red for the experimental group and green for controls). With tables, you can shade in the important blocks with a different color. All you need is your imagination. But don't let it run wild.

The more you practice making good overheads the better they will become. The skills you develop will be transferable to the use of more sophisticated computer programs and graphics packages if you ever encounter them. After all we are learning the basics of layout, organization and the communication of information when we design a simple overhead. And you thought you were just making a picture of the ear to show your class!

NOTES

Chapter Four

READING OR ROTE?

HOW DO I PRESENT MY TALK?

So, you've done all the work, organized your seminar and written it out. Now the big question: How do you present it? Should you simply read what you have written or should you use your notes as a guide and give your talk more-or-less by rote?

Few people enjoy amateur speeches. When you read your talk from a completely prepared text, more often than not you will end up giving a bad speech. Unless you are good at speeches or are a good actor, your talk will seem cold and sterile. When you make a mistake it will seem all the worst because, after all, isn't it all written down for you.

There's another problem with simply reading your talk. Sometimes people will interrupt your talk, causing you to lose your place. If you lose your place and then have difficulty continuing until you find exactly where you are, your audience will get the impression you do not know your material.

On the other side of the coin, we have the person who presents their talk totally by rote. Few people have such a good memory that they can give a complete seminar from memory. If a few major points are forgotten then your whole talk may seem disorganized or incoherent. If you remember such points later and interject them, your talk will seem disorganized.

USE CUE CARDS TO REMEMBER

The best talks are a combination of written information and rote. The written information serves as a cue to the sequence of topics. It can also provide solid facts in the form of specific quotes or other data. When you do run into trouble it can serve as a safety net.

Many students prefer to give talks using filing cards as cue cards. The major points are put on the front of the card and discussed. If you have trouble remembering certain points, they can be elaborated upon on the back of the card. In addition, the speaker can use the audio-visual aids as cues.

In the Introduction, the sequence of topics can be noted in point form and elaborated upon. In the Discussion, a graph can be projected and used to make specific points that are listed on a filing card. In short, the information you require is always available to you; not, however, as a sterile collection of sentences but as a sequence of points upon which you elaborate.

DON'T PANIC IF YOU FORGET SOMETHING

Sometimes a point will escape you for a moment or you might phrase something in a confusing way. If this happens, don't be afraid to stop and reorganize your thoughts. If you feel you might have confused your audience, rephrase the material with a lead-in phrase such as "Let me restate that" or "Let me clarify that point."

Thus part of your talk will be by rote. What it will not be is the simple memorization of an essay. Instead, you will know what points you are going to make but the way you say them may vary between your practice sessions and your final talk. This will instill a dynamic nature into your seminar. To drive this point home, examine how the news is presented on major networks versus small television stations. When you can tell someone is reading their material it is less alive, less sparkling.

WRITE DOWN YOUR INTRODUCTORY STATEMENTS

One extremely useful trick is to write the first few sentences of the Introduction out in full. Read these prepared sentences, then quickly shift into an audiovisual aid (e.g., an overhead) and speak to this projected material. This will get you off to a good start (your first few words will get your feet wet successfully) and then shift the audience's attention to something other than yourself (who at this point may be extremely nervous). Now your talk is underway in a positive way. You should also write down your concluding comments so you don't forget to say an important point.

WRITE DOWN IMPORTANT POINTS

In the heat of the moment, you may forget when it happened, who did what on which date and why. Make sure you avoid this problem by having all important information at your fingertips. Here are some things to remember in writing down information.

Write down:

- all important dates
- all important names
- any complex figures or numbers
- any words you have trouble with
- anything you are not sure about.

MAKE PHOTOCOPIES OF YOUR OVERHEADS

If you have lots of complex or detailed overheads there are some simple tricks you can use to keep from getting confused. Make an extra photocopy of your overheads on plain paper. Rather than making separate notes about what you will discuss when you show the overhead, write the points directly on the photocopy. In the case of the ear example discussed earlier, use a version of the original copy that still has the names printed on it. This will ensure the spelling and location of the structures will be correct.

If the overhead is used to make several points, list the points and number them so you will be sure to cover them in the proper order. If you need to clearly distinguish the points you could print them in different colors so they are easy to identify. On graphs and tables, you can go a step further by making the point and having an arrow indicate the specific part of the overhead you are referring to. Then when you put up the overhead, the arrow on the copy in your notes will remind you where to point.

In your notes, insert the copies of the annotated overheads exactly where they will be shown and discussed in your presentation. When you practice your talk having this information at your fingertips will make it easier for you to learn it. If you practice enough and know your material well, you probably won't have to refer to these pages during your presentation. It will help, however, knowing the information is at your fingertips if you do get nervous or confused.

Here's an example of how you could add directions to a graph you might show as an overhead:

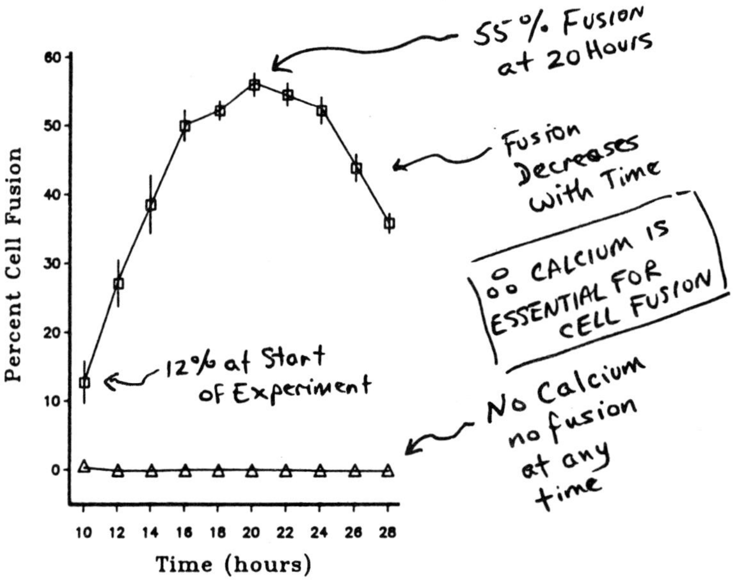

Chapter Five

IMPROVING YOUR TALK

MAKE IT INTERESTING

Every talk should tell a story. You want to grab then hold the audience's attention for the time allocated. No matter what the type of talk, it is essential that you make it interesting. A good speaker can take the driest material and make it interesting. Let's look at some ways to keep the interest of your audience.

USING HUMOR

Humor is never out place, no matter what some people will tell you. There is always a place for a sense of humor. The driest of talks can be revitalized with a touch of humor. Even the most sensitive subject can benefit from appropriate humor. Anyone who tells you differently probably lacks a sense of humor.

Humor doesn't mean telling jokes. While there are occasions when a joke may be appropriate or especially fitting to the situation, simply telling a joke to break the monotony usually seems contrived.

Here's an example of how a joke might be used. Imagine that were presenting a talk on surf boarding and you reached a point where you wanted to stress that the only way to become good at it was to practice. A classic joke, like this one, might fit the occasion:

"A young person with a violin case under her arm walked up to an old man on a New York street corner. 'Do you know the way to Carnegie Hall,' she asked. He replied, 'Practice, practice, practice.' You could then replay the punch line to make your point. "So, if you want to be a top-notch surfboarder, it takes practice, practice, practice."

There are so many reasons to practice your seminar that we could never list them all. But let's try to at least note a few of them.

THE IMPORTANCE OF PRACTICING

- To ensure your talk will be the right length
- To improve your timing so you don't rush
- To detect any problem areas that need work
- To gain confidence
- To learn to say difficult words and phrases
- To know your seminar
- To project an image of professionalism

HUMOR IS NOT JUST TELLING JOKES

Having said that humor is never out of place, it's best to avoid jokes in your talks. Instead use real anecdotes. With our surfboarding example, if you are really into the sport, you probably know of a real example where someone had to work hard to develop the necessary skills to be good. So, you would tell that story finishing with an example of how all of their floundering lead to winning a certain contest or making a spectacular move everyone talks about.

You can't tell people how to be funny. Some people have a well-developed sense of humor. They will have you laughing with a simple look or a few words. Others can take the funniest joke in the world and make you want to cry.

Humor is not necessarily being funny either. It is simply something that lightens the moment. Here's another example. A biologist was presenting his work on the ecology of a certain bird. The talk got very heavy after only a few minutes. Graph after graph of complex data started to put everyone to sleep. Then came the surprise: unexpected humor. A slide was presented that was very simple—a line with a few big dots or data points. As the speaker continued, the audience noticed that something was different about the graph. Very shortly, all of the data points rose in the air to the top of the screen. The seminar speaker followed this with the simple statement, "Well this data is still up in the air." Everyone laughed uproariously. (How did he do it? He put small lead beads on one half of the slide and covered it with Vaseline. Then he added the other side of the dual glass slide. When the slide projector heated up the slide, the Vaseline softened and the beads fell down. Since projectors show the image upside down, it looked like the beads went up into the air!) The trick was simple but effective. More importantly, it made everyone pay attention from that point on.

So, well-placed humor can be a useful tool. But don't push the issue. If the joke is lost on the audience or if the humor is not appropriate, then you could be worse off than if you were simply boring. The trick with the moving data points leads to another way to keep your talk interesting. While our seminar speaker used humor with his audiovisual aid, this isn't important. The point is that interesting and effective audiovisual aids are the mainstay of a good talk.

USING AUDIO-VISUAL AIDS EFFECTIVELY

As we discussed in Chapter Three, there is a wide array of audio-visual aids available. Most students do not have the time, money or expertise to make their own 35mm slides or to produce elaborate graphics for class talks. In the same vein, we can rule out videotaping as a routine mode of audio-visual communication. These techniques will be used by some students, but usually only in specialty courses.

The main means of communicating audio-visual information will be via your own voice and a blackboard. White boards with colored pens are also becoming common. Other major means of communication will be via the use of an overhead or opaque projector, and using photocopied handouts. Used sensibly, these means of augmenting your oral presentation can turn an average talk into one that is first-rate. We discussed the mechanics of preparing excellent overheads in Chapter Three. Using them properly is another issue. At this point we're going to discuss how to use these techniques effectively.

If you want your audience to be continually aware of where you are going, or if certain points are going to be raised over and over, you would be wise to list these on the blackboard. Then you can simply refer to them with a well-directed point of your hand throughout your presentation. Too often speakers use an overhead that they must continually refer back to. As they progress through their other overheads, the orientation list gets lost in the shuffle. It would be easier in such cases to simply list the points on the board where they will serve as a continual reminder to their audience. If you decide to use one overhead to orient your readers, make sure it doesn't get buried and check off the points as you cover them.

As you continue your talk you can also add new material to the list or add names, dates or whatever to the information that's already there. In this way, the board becomes a dynamic, integral part of your talk and can help lead your audience to your final conclusions.

USING OVERHEADS EFFECTIVELY

Overheads are a simple and potentially dramatic way of presenting visual information. The main problem with overheads is knowing how much information to convey and how to convey it. Here, we'll give you more comments on how to use overheads effectively, Some of this repeats a few points made earlier, but in a different way. You should refer back to Chapter Three for more details on the mechanics of overhead production. In using overheads it is important to keep the following points in mind:

Less is More

The concept "less is more" applies here. Speakers have a tendency to write down detailed points in fine hand-writing either because they are afraid that they will forget things or because they want to save a nickel. This approach is tedious and produces visual aids that generally are unreadable. As in writing on the blackboard, put down any points as succinctly as possible and print in large letters that are easily visible at the back of the seminar room.

Don't Just Copy Anything as an Overhead

Remember authors do not write their books with undergraduate seminars in mind. Therefore they may include material that is essential in the context of their work but useless or confusing in the context of your talk. If you are making overheads from textbook information, decide whether or not you should make your own notes, tables or diagrams on an overhead sheet, leaving out the irrelevant information. If you decide to use a complex chart, table or figure from a text, you can enhance the information content by using colored markers to outline the important sequence, information or line.

One Overhead, One Graph, One Figure

Don't try to cram several sets of data onto a single overhead. Use a single overhead for each set of information and then, if it is necessary, you might have a final composite overhead to demonstrate the inter-relationships between the material. If you intend to make an overhead from a page that contains text or other extraneous information, make a photocopy of that page first. Then cut out the extraneous material and use the cleaned up copy to make your overhead. It not only is easier to look at, it looks more professional.

Use Copies of Your Overheads as Handouts

These points also apply to making photocopies for handouts. If you photocopy material, cut out the relevant material and repaste it alone or with other material on a piece of paper for recopying. For a handout you can include more material per page than you should for an overhead. Just make sure the sequence and nature of each part is indicated. The value of handing out the information is that the students can then pay more attention to what is being said rather than panicking if they have write it all down. They can use the handouts to add extra information from your talk if the teacher expects them to. Everyone enjoys getting something when they go to a talk, so a well-prepared handout can give the audience a positive feeling about your talk before you even begin.

MORE HELPFUL HINTS FOR USING OVERHEADS

Here are a few more important points:

- Point to specific items as you mention them: Don't just wave your hand at the overhead.
- Use different wording on your overhead than you do in your talk
- Don't just read an overhead; discuss it.
- Leave your overhead up long enough for your audience to read and understand them.
- For long lists of points, check off items as you cover them.

Chapter Five

A SHORT REVIEW

PRESENTING A TALK: SUMMARY

1. Oral presentations come in many formats from a simple summary of a topic to a full-fledged seminar or talk.

2. A seminar or class talk consists of three elements:

- Introduction. Sets the stage for what you are going to talk about
- Discussion. Gives the evidence leading up to your conclusions
- Conclusion. Summarizes the points you have made with overall summation of ideas

3. Oral presentations should be logical progressions of ideas.

4. It is up to you to decide whether you will read a fully prepared talk or give it solely by rote. The best talks come somewhere in the middle with some of the material read and other aspects reflected on spontaneously.

5. Speak clearly and at a moderate pace.

6. Use humor sparingly and wisely. Avoid jokes.

7. Overhead projectors can be used effectively to:

- Present an overview of what will be covered
- Keep you on track
- Present graphic and tabular data
- Keep your audience interested

8. In presenting information on overheads be succinct. Too much information is confusing.

ORDER INFORMATION

Use the following form (plus check or money order)
or, send a purchase order to:

Canada:
TRILOBYTE PRESS
1486 Willowdown Road
Oakville, ON L6L 1X3

USA:
TRILOBYTE PRESS
Unit 443, 825 E Roosevelt Rd
Lombard, IL 60148

Or, **FAX** Your Order:

(416) 847-3258

(708) 916-1148

Quantity	**Item**	**Cost**
	How to Succeed at College ($12.95 US; $14.95 Canada)	
	How to Succeed at University ($11.95 Canada only)	
	Student Time Manager ($12.95 US; $14.95 Canada)	
	Basic Concepts Learning Guides© ($3.95 US; $4.95 Canada each) How to Study & Learn How to Write Tests & Exams How to Write Reports & Essays How to Give a Classroom Talk How to Plan & Get Organized How to Write Resumes & Cover Letters How to Find That Job	
Subtotal		
Shipping & Handling ($3.00 or 5%, whichever is greater)		
GST (add 7%; Canada only)		
TOTAL AMOUNT DUE		